Essential Issues

DOMESTIC VIOLENCE

Essential Issues

Domestic Violence

BY KAREN LATCHANA KENNEY

Content Consultant
Darald Hanusa
Senior Lecturer & Preceptor
School of Social Work, University of Wisconsin–Madison

ABDO
Publishing Company

CREDITS

Published by ABDO Publishing Company, 8000 West 78th Street, Edina, Minnesota 55439. Copyright © 2012 by Abdo Consulting Group, Inc. International copyrights reserved in all countries. No part of this book may be reproduced in any form without written permission from the publisher. The Essential Library™ is a trademark and logo of ABDO Publishing Company.

Printed in the United States of America,
North Mankato, Minnesota
062011
092011

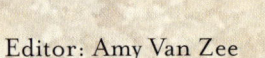 THIS BOOK CONTAINS AT LEAST 10% RECYCLED MATERIALS.

Editor: Amy Van Zee
Copy Editor: Jennifer Joline Anderson
Design and Production: Marie Tupy

Library of Congress Cataloging-in-Publication Data
Kenney, Karen Latchana.
  Domestic violence / by Karen Latchana Kenney.
    p. cm. -- (Essential issues)
  Includes bibliographical references and index.
  ISBN 978-1-61783-133-1
  1. Family violence--Juvenile literature. I. Title.
  HV6626.K46 2012
  362.82'92--dc22
                              2011016516

Domestic Violence

TABLE OF CONTENTS

Chapter 1	A Murderous Rage	6
Chapter 2	The Origins of Domestic Violence	16
Chapter 3	The Victims	26
Chapter 4	The Abusers	36
Chapter 5	Lasting Effects	46
Chapter 6	A Global Issue	56
Chapter 7	Law Enforcement and the Legal System	66
Chapter 8	Advocacy and Legislation	76
Chapter 9	Breaking the Cycle	86

Timeline	96
Essential Facts	100
Glossary	102
Additional Resources	104
Source Notes	106
Index	109
About the Author	112

Chapter 1

A T-shirt is displayed as part of a 2011 event intended to raise awareness about the dangers of domestic and dating violence.

A Murderous Rage

It was a clear summer evening, the end of a beautiful Saturday in June 2007. Residents of the quiet town of Delavan, Wisconsin, drifted to sleep. They had no idea of the tragedy they would wake up to the next day.

Domestic Violence

That night, June 9, a 911 dispatcher received a chilling call just after 10:30 p.m. "I was inside of my house and my sister-in-law, her boyfriend came in and started shooting everybody," said the male caller.[1] The caller was Gaspar Huerta, who had escaped the gunfire by crawling through a window and making a desperate call for help. The dispatcher asked, "He's shooting your wife and kids? So he's at the house now?"[2] The shooter was still there, and Huerta pleaded for the police to "please hurry up please. He's there shooting my wife and all their kids."[3]

Police soon arrived to find a horrific scene at the white duplex. A two-year-old girl named Jasmine Analco was found inside a car parked in front of the house. The girl had been shot in the chest but was still alive. Jasmine was quickly rushed to the hospital for emergency treatment. Upstairs in the duplex, police found the remaining victims and the murderer. It was a tragic sight. All were dead—four adults and two twin baby boys. The victims were 19-year-old Nicole Marie McAffee, her one-year-old twins, Argenis and Isaiah Analco, 21-year-old Ashley Lynn Huerta (sister to Nicole and wife of Gaspar Huerta), and 19-year-old Vanessa L. Iverson, a family friend.

The murderer was 23-year-old Ambrosio Analco, father to Jasmine, Argenis, and Isaiah Analco, and ex-boyfriend of Nicole McAffee, who was the children's mother. He had taken his own life after killing everyone inside the home.

Previous Threats

Police immediately suspected that it was a case of domestic violence, but they had not received previous calls from the house. However, this was not the first time Ambrosio Analco had been violent with his girlfriend, Nicole McAffee. Jose Huerta, the brother of the 911 caller, had once seen bruises on McAffee's face. "She said (Analco) was the one who punched her," Huerta recalled. "I told her to go to the police. She didn't say nothing. He told her he was going to kill her."[4]

Ashley Huerta, Nicole McAffee's sister and one of the victims killed that day, also knew of Analco's violent tendencies. Ashley had once told her brother-in-law, Victor, about Analco's threat. Victor said, "When I was there, [Ashley] said that supposedly the guy said if [Nicole] cheated with another guy, he's going to kill her and everybody in the house."[5] The threats were not taken seriously,

Domestic Violence

though, and Analco was still allowed to visit McAffee's home.

McAffee's father never knew there was any problem with Analco. His daughter had kept the abuse a secret from him, and he learned only after the murders that Analco was a heavy drinker and had made threats. Neighbors, too, were shocked by the event. They said they had rarely heard any disturbances and everything had seemed fairly normal at the home.

Beyond the Tragedy

Analco and McAffee had lived together, but there were problems in the relationship

Domestic Violence Awareness Month

On the first day of October, the Day of Unity is celebrated as the start of Domestic Violence Awareness Month. The Day of Unity was first observed in 1981 by the National Coalition Against Domestic Violence (NCADV) as a way to bring together battered women's advocates from around the United States. In the following years, the day stretched into a week of activities. Participants mourned the deaths of domestic abuse victims, celebrated the survivors, and connected with others working for the cause.

The first Domestic Violence Awareness Month was observed in 1987. Also that year, a national toll-free hotline was created for victims. In 1989, the US Congress passed legislation commemorating the month. In October 1994, the NCADV and *Ms.* magazine created the "Remember My Name" project, a national registry of women killed by an intimate partner. The project aims to increase public awareness of deaths caused by domestic violence in the United States. Today, the Day of Unity and Domestic Violence Awareness Month are observed in communities across the country.

and the couple had recently split up. At the time of the murders, McAffee lived in the duplex with her children, her sister Ashley, and her sister's husband Gaspar Huerta. On the day of the murders, Analco had taken his three children to visit his cousin. He then returned to McAffee's home at 9:00 p.m. McAffee's friend Vanessa Iverson was there visiting. The murders occurred sometime between 9:00 p.m. and 10:30 p.m. Neighbors awoke the next day to the crime scene and were shocked to hear of the tragedy. Outside the duplex, mourners placed flowers, teddy bears, and candles in memory of the lost lives.

Young Jasmine Analco survived her gunshot wound. Now an orphan, she is being raised by her grandparents. Gaspar Huerta struggles with depression since the murders of his wife and family members. He tried to commit suicide but survived, although with permanent injuries. In a television interview two years after his painful experience, Huerta urged people to fight against domestic violence.

What Is Domestic Violence?

Domestic violence affects people of all cultures, ages, and economic and educational backgrounds.

Domestic Violence

It is a type of violence that occurs between family members and intimate partners when one person tries to control another. The victim might be a wife, husband, child, or elderly family member. Most often, though, domestic violence is committed by men against women. The abuser's behavior can include physical, psychological, and sexual methods of control. Noticeable effects might be a black eye or a broken arm. But there is much more to domestic violence than the visible signs.

For intimate partners, emotional abuse can include humiliation, forced isolation, and loss of control over finances. The abuser may drive recklessly or make threats with weapons to scare the victim. He or she may also try to control the victim with intense jealousy, call the victim degrading names, and sexually harass or rape the victim. Victims who are

Female Victims

According to the NCADV, women make up 85 percent of domestic violence victims in the United States. One in every four women will experience domestic violence at some point in her life.

Essential Issues

> "Domestic violence causes far more pain than the visible marks of bruises and scars. It is devastating to be abused by someone that you love and think loves you in return. It is estimated that approximately 3 million incidents of domestic violence are reported each year in the United States. Tragically, domestic violence remains a pervasive threat to the fabric of America's families and the well-being of America's future."[6]
>
> —US Senator Dianne Feinstein, in her October 6, 2004, statement to the 108th Congress on *Domestic Violence in America*

abused by the ones they love become intimidated and fearful in their own homes and can feel powerless to stop the violence.

Domestic violence also impacts the lives of children in the home. Statistics can be difficult to pin down, but it is estimated that 3 to 10 million children witness a parent suffering from intimate partner violence every year. Abusive parents can also physically, emotionally, or sexually abuse their children. As a result, children may exhibit signs of depression, anxiety, aggression, and other serious emotional and behavioral problems. When a home becomes an unsafe environment for children, they also feel helpless and insecure.

Domestic violence can also include violence against elders, but not all elder abuse is domestic violence. Elder abuse that is considered domestic violence is violence against an aged family member. As they age, elderly people may need help with daily tasks, such as paying bills, bathing, or preparing

Domestic Violence

Advocates gathered at a rally in Kentucky that aimed to stop elder abuse.

food. This leaves them vulnerable to physical, sexual, financial, or emotional abuse by family members or other caregivers. Family members can also neglect an elder by not providing food, water, or other basic necessities. Often, elderly people are too ill to ask for help or leave the home, making them unable to escape the abuse.

Domestic violence is a global issue; it affects families around the world. The violence may begin small with a push, a slap, or a kick. If the violence escalates, its consequences can be deadly, as in Delavan, Wisconsin. Homicide is sometimes an end

Essential Issues

result of domestic violence. In the United States, approximately one-third of all female homicide victims are killed by an intimate partner. Living with violent family members puts children and the elderly at risk for abuse and its lasting physical and mental effects. For example, children who witness family violence are at risk of becoming violent or becoming abuse victims later in life.

Domestic abuse typically happens behind closed doors. It is a crime that is not always reported to the police. Many times neighbors and friends do not realize the abuse is happening. Unless visible physical signs are present, it is difficult to know what occurs in someone's home. With advocacy, legislation, and public education, the issue of domestic violence can be brought out into the open, helping more victims escape abuse and ensuring that abusers are tried for their crimes.

Verbal Abuse

Many domestic abuse cases involve verbal abuse. It can be subtle and difficult to define, but years of verbal abuse can cause significant emotional damage. Types of verbal abuse include:

- Accusing a partner of being unfaithful
- Calling a partner names
- Ignoring a partner
- Withholding approval or affection as a punishment
- Saying "You're stupid" or "You're ugly"
- Humiliating a partner in public or in front of family
- Threatening to harm children, family, or friends
- Leaving nasty or harassing voice mail messages

Domestic Violence

Carolyn Thomas was shot in the face by her boyfriend in 2003.
She now speaks publicly about domestic violence.

Chapter 2

Frances Power Cobbe lived from 1822 to 1904. She studied and wrote about violence against women.

The Origins of Domestic Violence

For thousands of years, violence against women and children has not only been tolerated and accepted as normal practice, but it has also been encouraged. In patriarchal societies around the world, women and children have long

Domestic Violence

been considered to be subservient family members, while males have held dominant roles. Society and laws have often upheld a man's right to control his family, even by using violence, from ancient times to the present day.

Patriarchy is a type of social organization that places the father as the supreme ruler within a family, making the wife and children dependent upon him by law and societal expectation. In a patriarchal society, women and children are viewed as the property of husbands. Women are also viewed as being inferior to men on many levels: intellectually, emotionally, physically, sexually, and spiritually. Domestic violence is rooted in this view of male dominance within families and in societies that do not value women's rights.

Ancient Times

In most ancient societies, women were treated as the property of their fathers and then of their husbands. Paying a father a "bride price" for

---

Family

In modern English, the word *family* has a positive connotation as a term describing a group of people related to each other. Originally, however, the word *family* meant "servants of a household." The word comes from the Latin *familia*, used by ancient Romans to describe the group of slaves owned by a man. This expression was then used to describe a social unit headed by a man who had a wife, children, and several slaves. According to Roman law, the man had the right to control the life and death of members of his *familia*.

his daughter was a common way for a man to find his wife. If the family was poor, daughters were often sold into prostitution as well as marriage.

Ancient Greece, for instance, was a typical patriarchal society. Women had few legal rights and depended upon their husbands for support. Women's main function in society was to bear male heirs for their husbands and to take care of their homes. Greek philosopher Aristotle expressed the common view of women at the time:

> *The male is by nature superior, and the female inferior; and the one rules, and the other is ruled; this principle, of necessity, extends to all mankind. . . . The courage of a man is shown in commanding, of a woman in obeying.*[1]

"In a number of cases men may be excused for the injuries they inflict on their wives, nor should the law intervene. Provided he neither kills nor maims her, it is legal for a man to beat his wife when she wrongs him."[2]
—The Laws and Customs of Beauvais, *a French legal code from the thirteenth century CE*

Society in many early cultures excluded women from roles outside the family. Women were not permitted to be involved in government and were excluded from studying science, law, and philosophy. Often they were excluded from religious roles as well.

In ancient Rome, women also had few legal rights and were not citizens.

Domestic Violence

The head of the household, a father or a husband, could decide the fate of his family members. Baby girls were not considered to be as valuable as boys, who could eventually work to support their families. Many times, newborn girls were rejected by the head and left outside the home to die or be rescued by a stranger. Laws gave Roman husbands the right to beat, divorce, or kill their wives for a variety of offenses. For instance, women could be punished for drinking wine, attending public games without the permission of their husbands, or walking outside with their faces uncovered.

Frances Power Cobbe

Victorian feminist Frances Power Cobbe was born in 1822 in the town of Newbridge, Ireland. Being from a wealthy family, Cobbe was educated by governesses and attended a private girls' school. She read widely as a young woman and especially enjoyed the writings of German philosopher Immanuel Kant.

As an adult, Cobbe moved to England and became involved in charity work, mostly with workhouse children. Her work among the poor opened her eyes to domestic abuse suffered by women. In 1878, Cobbe wrote a pamphlet entitled "Wife Torture in England," which examines 6,000 cases of domestic violence, including cases in which women had been maimed, blinded, trampled, burned, and murdered. Cobbe linked women's economic dependence on men with domestic violence, stating that economic power was one way for a man to completely control his wife.

Cobbe's work influenced the Matrimonial Causes Act of 1878, which awarded abused wives the ability to separate from their husbands, keep custody of their children, and receive financial support after separation.

Medieval Europe and Early Feminism

During the medieval period in Europe (from the fifth to the fifteenth centuries), men were encouraged by the church to be the moral guardians of women and were permitted by law to punish them with violence for any offenses committed. Through the seventeenth and eighteenth centuries, violence against women was an accepted aspect of society. In the American colonies, judges usually sided with husbands in domestic violence cases in accordance with English common law, which allowed certain types of violence against wives.

In the eighteenth century, voices in opposition of domestic violence began to be heard publicly. These voices were the earliest traces of the feminist movement, which stood for the equal political, social, and economic rights of women. This movement challenged the patriarchy by asserting that women were not inferior to men and should not be dominated by men. In 1792, British writer Mary Wollstonecraft wrote one of the first books advocating for women's rights, *A Vindication of the Rights of Woman*. In the book, Wollstonecraft suggests that the equal treatment of women and the ability to educate themselves would benefit women, men, and society as a whole.

Domestic Violence

Mary Wollstonecraft advocated for better educational opportunities for women.

Other voices joined the movement to fight for women's rights, including the right to vote and have equal educational and employment opportunities.

Essential Issues

An 1847 etching depicts the violent effects of alcohol abuse on men, women, and children.

In the late 1800s, John Stuart Mill published *The Subjection of Women*, which calls for an end to wife abuse. Mill wrote not only about physical violence against women, but he also wrote about the legal and psychological effects of the male dominance of women.

Also in the late 1800s, groups formed to protect children from domestic violence. These societies tried to stay out of husband-wife relations, though, and they instead focused on child abuse and neglect. Many battered women turned to these agencies for help, as there were no agencies focused on abused wives.

Battered Women's Movement

In the United States, from the 1920s until the late 1950s, numerous social and political issues dominated the culture. In some ways, the women's rights movement faded from public view. But the civil rights movement of the 1950s and 1960s, which led to greater African-American equality in the United States, paved the way for the modern feminist movement. Feminism again gained momentum and led to the battered women's movement in the 1970s. Women spoke publicly about the abuse happening in their homes. Around the world, stories of domestic violence raised the public's awareness of this widespread issue.

State v. Jesse Black

In 1864, the Supreme Court of North Carolina ruled in the case of the *State v. Jesse Black* that a man had the right to abuse his wife if she called him names. The judgment read:

"A husband is responsible for the acts of his wife, and he is required to govern his household, and for that purpose the law permits him to use towards his wife such a degree of force as is necessary to control an unruly temper and make her behave herself; and unless some permanent injury be inflicted, or there be excess of violence, or such a degree of cruelty as shows that it is inflicted to gratify his own bad passions, the law will not invade the domestic forum or go behind the curtain."[3]

Essential Issues

Domestic abuse was no longer a private, family matter.

In response, feminists and other women's advocates created services to assist victims of domestic violence. They established shelters, safe houses, and crisis hotlines throughout the United States. The NCADV and other groups held national conferences focusing on domestic violence to educate the public and allow activists to share information. The issue received national attention and advocates lobbied public officials to take action. The government responded with several pieces of legislation establishing support services to victims of domestic violence. By speaking out, victims have brought the issue of domestic violence into the open. Knowing about the issue enables friends, family, and the public to take action if they see the signs of abuse.

Violence against Men

Throughout history, little has been written about domestic violence against men. Although it has certainly existed, it was historically considered a shameful secret. It was thought best to maintain the appearance of male dominance in a couple's relationship. A common practice in England from the fifteenth through the nineteenth centuries proved this view. There, when a man was found to be a victim of his wife's violence, he might be paraded through town on the back of a donkey as part of a humiliating custom known as a "skimmington." The man would be ridiculed for letting his private life become public knowledge.

Domestic Violence

The battered women's movement gained momentum in a few countries. In 1975, English women protested the lack of shelters for abused wives.

Chapter 3

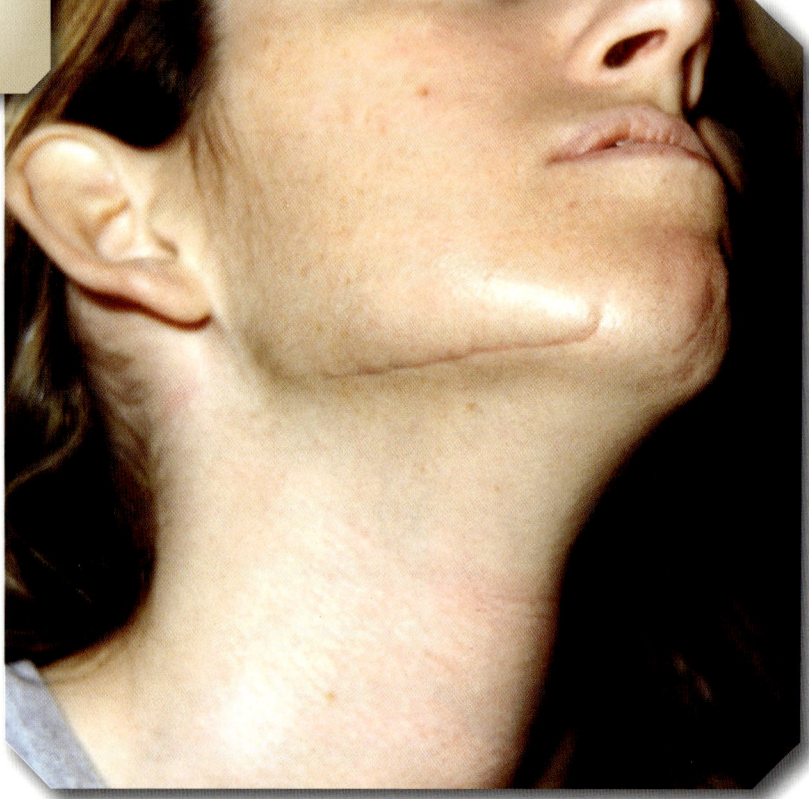

Michelle Comeau shows her jawline scar. She was stabbed by her boyfriend in 1999.

The Victims

Any given crowd could consist of mothers, fathers, children, and elderly people. They might appear wealthy, middle class, or poor. Each might be from a different ethnic background. Any one of those people might be a

Domestic Violence

victim of abuse. It is not easy to spot a victim of domestic violence.

Abusive people often attack family members because they are easily accessible. The abuser need only walk down the hallway and open the door to the victim's bedroom. And behind the protective walls of a home, abusers can commit their abuse without being seen.

Intimate Partner Abuse

Marriage is a close relationship in which couples commit to loving and caring for their partner. But spouses and intimate partners are often prime targets of domestic violence. Women ages 20–24 are at the highest risk for this abuse.

Domestic abuse occurs when a person attempts to control his or her spouse or domestic partner. It may start with emotional abuse. This abuse works to diminish a victim's self-esteem and make a victim dependent on the abuser. The emotional abuse can be verbal, such as yelling or name-calling. Abusers may offer threats by saying they will commit physical harm to the victim, the victim's family members, or even the victim's pets. Emotional abuse can also include financial control. A victim may not be allowed to work or have a bank account. Abusers may dole out an allowance of a certain amount every month and have victims account for every dime they spend.

Digital abuse, also known as cyberbullying, is another way in which abusers harm their victims. Digital abuse includes unwanted instant messages or texts. The messages might be harassing or threatening. One person might pressure the other to participate in "sexting," which means sending naked photos or sexually explicit texts over the phone, against his or her will. Or a partner could visit social networking pages to leave threatening messages or spread rumors about the partner.

The abuse usually becomes physical. This is when a partner uses his or her superior strength or size to hurt the victim. At first the abuse may be minor, such as pinching or hair pulling, so that the victim might think the abuse is not that bad. But then the violence escalates. It can include punching or kicking, abandoning the victim in a dangerous place, or pinning the victim against the floor or a wall. In some cases, the physical abuse includes the use of weapons, such as knives or guns, which can lead to deadly results. Abusers may also break victims' personal items or punch holes in walls or doors.

Domestic Violence

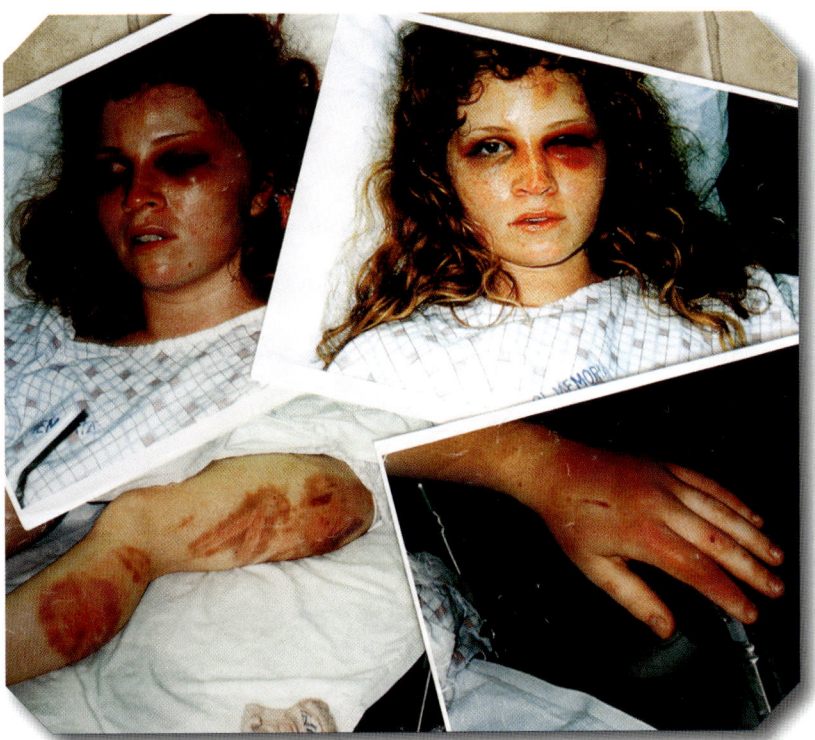

Heather Thompson was beaten by her husband in 1994. He spent time in prison for his crimes and later vowed to kill her and their daughters.

If physical abuse is occurring in a relationship, it is likely there is also sexual abuse. Sexual abuse is when abusers use sexual acts to control, humiliate, or demean their partners. It can include unwanted touching, hurting a partner during sex, or raping a partner. In the past, it was widely believed that a married man had the right to sex, even without his wife's consent. Until the 1970s, marital rape was not

Essential Issues

considered a crime in most states. Today, however, US law recognizes that even if two people are married, one partner does not have the right to force the other to participate in sexual acts.

Victim Reactions

When abuse occurs, especially by a loved one, the victim often changes his or her behavior to keep safe. For instance, a victim may become withdrawn and quiet, knowing that discussing certain topics upsets the abuser. The victim will often appear overly anxious to please the abusive partner and may lose contact with friends and avoid social gatherings because of the abuser's extreme jealousy. He or she may miss work or have frequent unexplained injuries.

After repetitive abuse, victims suffer from low self-esteem and depression. Some may even begin thinking the abuse is deserved or that they caused the abuse to happen—although in reality this is

Safety Plans

In a violent relationship, it is important for victims to create safety plans. A safety plan is a plan of quick escape during a violent episode. Parts of a safety plan include:

• Having a safe place to go, which could include a friend's home or a shelter

• Packing a suitcase ahead of time with extra clothes, extra keys, and personal items

• Keeping important items, such as credit cards or a checkbook, in one spot, so they are easy to take in a hurry

• Talking to children to explain what they should do in a violent situation

• Going to an emergency room or doctor when injured

• Calling the police to report the violent incident

impossible, because a person has no control over a partner's behavior. As the abuse continues, victims feel helpless to stop it and become passive and submissive. They may also go into a state of denial, convincing themselves the abuse is not that bad or that it is not occurring at all.

Spouses or domestic partners may stay in abusive relationships because they believe that surviving outside the relationship is impossible, both financially and emotionally. Suffering from low self-esteem and depression, they often believe they are incapable of finding jobs or living independently. They may also have nowhere else to go. With little money, they cannot pay for a hotel room or other temporary shelter. Another reason victims stay with abusive partners is to protect other family members from abuse. A victim does not want to leave children and elders in the care of the abuser. And in many cases, victims stay because they believe the abusers will find them and severely hurt or kill them if they leave the relationship.

Child and Elder Abuse

Much of the same type of abuse spouses suffer can also be aimed at children and the elderly. But, since children and some elders are completely dependent upon family members, abuse can also include neglect. This is the denial of basic necessities, such as food, water, or clothing. And, if domestic violence is present in the home, the risk that children will be physically, sexually, or emotionally abused or neglected is 15 times higher than the national average.

For children—who are still developing physically, mentally, and emotionally—domestic violence can be a devastating

> **A Victim's Story**
>
> Julie J. is a victim of spousal abuse. Her story is told through the Domestic Violence Resource Center:
>
> *I caught my partner in another lie. He went ballistic. He threw things at me, he broke windows, he pushed me, he slapped my face, he strangled me so I could not breathe, he threatened to tie me up because I would go to the police and then he pulled out a carving knife and held it over my head, screaming that I knew too much and he would have to kill me. I begged for my life. He began to deescalate and then quickly fell asleep. . . .*
>
> *I did not leave until the next morning. I was scared, I was ashamed, and I was in shock that this had ever happened to me. . . . My child and my boss convinced me to call the police. I did not make that call for two days.*
>
> *I got a restraining order against him. . . . Later, [my husband] appeared in court, pleaded guilty, three of four charges were dropped, and he ended up with a misdemeanor charge. [My husband] has not only violated the judgment numerous times, but he has also violated the restraining order. I live in fear that he may kidnap me and torture me.*[1]

event that shapes the adults they will become. Whether children witness domestic violence or are the targets of abuse, they may suffer the same lasting effects. They can suffer immediate consequences, which include physical injuries and anxiety. Long-term effects include brain damage from being shaken. Psychological damage, such as the inability to form close relationships with others, can also occur. Children know little of life outside their own families, so they often believe that violence and abuse are normal. This puts children at a higher risk to continue the cycle of violence as adults by either becoming abusers or victims.

Signs of child abuse can be seen at school or in other public places. Children may become withdrawn, or they might suddenly have little interest in schoolwork and begin receiving poor grades. They may also

Helping an Abuse Victim

The National Domestic Violence Hotline offers the following advice for helping someone in an abusive relationship:

• Express concern to the victim and explain why the relationship seems unhealthy.

• Acknowledge that the victim is in a frightening situation and that it is not his or her fault.

• Explain that there are agencies and shelters available to support victims of abuse.

• Listen to and be supportive of the victim. Understand that it may be hard for him or her to talk about the relationship.

• Do not judge. Be accepting of the victim's decisions.

• Encourage the victim to go out and do things with friends and family.

• Support the victim if he or she ends the relationship. Know that the victim may feel sad or mourn the relationship.

• Help the victim develop a safety plan.

begin acting violently by fighting with or threatening their peers. Teachers, friends, or school nurses might be able to spot the signs of child abuse. Elder abuse, however, can be difficult to notice. Elders may be unable to leave the home without help or may have mental ailments that prevent them from recognizing and telling others about the abuse. It can also be difficult to tell whether changes in an elder's appearance or attitude are due to common ailments of aging, such as dementia or Alzheimer's disease, or whether they are signs of abuse.

If elders are being neglected, they may rapidly lose weight or appear unwashed and unclean. They may have unexplained broken bones or suffer from a prescription drug overdose as the result of physical abuse. Financial exploitation is also a component of elder abuse. Caregivers may steal elders' savings or social security payments. Elders may have no way to escape violent homes on their own. They must stay unless a friend or outside family member intervenes.

Domestic Violence

A 2003 US postage stamp features a drawing by a child. The stamp raised money for programs fighting domestic violence.

Chapter 4

Robert Steven Hatch went on trial in 2003 for the murder of his estranged wife. Charges also included robbery and domestic violence.

THE ABUSERS

An abuser may seem average, friendly, or even charming in public. He or she may be a successful businessperson or a reliable coworker. Often, family members are the only people who see an abuser's violent side.

Domestic Violence

Abusers often know how to hide their abusive actions. Even if angry, they typically wait to commit the abuse in private. They might hit their victims in places on the body that are easily hidden by clothing, such as the arms or legs. They often change moods suddenly, switching from a calm demeanor to a crazy, out-of-control rage. While abusers can be men or women, there are certain characteristics that abusers share. Most follow a typical cycle of abuse.

Warning Signs

At the beginning of a relationship, abusers might seem like the perfect partners. They are loving and complimentary. They express strong feelings and push for a quick commitment. As the relationship progresses, however, the partner may start noticing signs of potential problems. Jealousy is common, and abusers will call their partners constantly and interrogate them about where they have been or who they have seen. After a while, the abuser tries to isolate the partner from friends and

Same-Sex Relationships

Abuse happens in heterosexual relationships, but it also occurs between same-sex couples. According to a report by the National Violence Against Women Survey, "11% of lesbians reported violence by their female partner and 15% of gay men who had lived with a male partner reported being victimized by a male partner."[1]

family. This way, the abuser can more easily control the partner. A partner may be prevented from working or have his or her money taken away. The abuser may be unkind to children by cruelly teasing or punishing them. An abuser might also harm animals—kicking, hitting, or even killing pets.

Deeper into the relationship, the abuser will emotionally abuse a victim and blame that person for his or her rage. Then the physical abuse and violent threats begin. As this happens, abusers remain in a state of denial. Sometimes they minimize the violence by stating that it was only a slap or a push.

Stalking

During a relationship or after a relationship ends, an abuser may begin stalking the victim—that is, following or harassing the person with unwanted visits or calls. Over time, stalking can become more violent and obsessive. Abusers may threaten to harm or kill the victim, causing the victim to live in a constant state of fear.

Some stalkers are strangers to the victim, but it is far more common for a person to be stalked by a current or former romantic partner. According to a survey by the US Department of Justice,

> Women tend to be stalked by intimate partners, defined as current or former spouses, current or former cohabitants (of the same or opposite sex), or current or former boyfriends or girlfriends. Thirty-eight percent of female stalking victims were stalked by current or former husbands, 10 percent by current or former cohabiting partners, and 14 percent by current or former dates or boyfriends. Overall, 59 percent of female victims, compared with 30 percent of male victims, were stalked by some type of intimate partner.[2]

Domestic Violence

Other times they claim it happened because they lost control and it was not their fault. They may even deny the abuse happened at all and attempt to convince the victim that it was imagined. By the time the abuse is an expected pattern of behavior, the relationship has been going on for some time. There may be children involved and deep emotional ties in the relationship.

Why Are They Abusive?

An abuser wants to control his or her partner. Why? Low self-esteem, a feeling of loss of power in one's life, and a belief that using violence against a partner is acceptable are all contributing factors. If a couple is experiencing financial strain, such as sudden job loss, the abusive person may respond with violence in an effort to restore his or her sense of control. In the case of elder abuse, money may also be a motivator, as family caregivers find ways to steal an elder's savings or income.

Growing up in a home where violence is witnessed or felt is a predictor of future violent behavior. Abusers may also learn violent behavior through their friends, culture, or community. They may believe that the only way to make a partner stay

Essential Issues

Female Batterers

Women can also be guilty of abusing men or other women. Male victims of domestic abuse may be less likely to report the abuse to law enforcement due to the fear of being perceived as weak or unmanly.

Women who use violence do not always do so for the same reasons as men who use violence. According to the Center Against Rape and Domestic Violence, "Studies show that the majority of women who abuse male partners have been previously abused by these male partners and are now using violence in an effort to get them to stop. The next largest group of female batterers were women who had been abused by some other male partner in their past and now wanted to [ensure] that no one would ever physically harm them again. The smallest group of female batterers were those who battered for the same reason males batter—in order to gain power and control over their partner."[3]

is by controlling the partner. But inevitably, this behavior drives the victim away from the relationship. Or in worst cases, the partner dies at the hands of an abuser or fights back and kills the abuser.

Many abusers become depressed or full of rage when their partners leave. Although they mistreat them, abusers are dependent upon their partners. They need to control another person to feel better about themselves. During the separation, abusers may threaten suicide or murder. They apologize for the violence and promise to change. They may even appear to have changed for a while, but inevitably the cycle of abuse begins again.

The Cycle of Abuse

Violent relationships are not constantly violent. There are times of calm, times of extreme violence, and times of remorse. The cycle

Domestic Violence

feeds itself, perpetuating the violence in an abusive relationship. While all relationships are different, in violent relationships, it is common for a pattern to emerge.

There are six main phases in the cycle of a violent relationship. The abuse is one phase of the cycle. After the abuse, the batterer enters the guilt stage. He or she apologizes, promising not to repeat the abuse. But the abuser does not feel genuinely guilty about the partner's suffering; instead, the abuser is worried about possible consequences or punishment. By apologizing to the victim, the abuser gains control of the situation again, ensuring that the victim will not leave or tell others about the abuse.

Abusers then enter the rationalization phase, during which they make excuses for their violent behavior. Rather than take responsibility for what they have done, they may make the excuse that they were intoxicated or that they were abused as a child. They may also argue that the victim caused them to enter a rage by saying or doing something wrong.

Next is the "back to normal" phase. The relationship may seem great at this time. The abuser often buys gifts and takes the victim out for meals in an attempt to convince the victim that he or she

Essential Issues

will change and the relationship will be different. When things start to seem safe again, the abuser enters the planning and fantasizing phase. Here, the abuser focuses on what the partner has done wrong and what the abuser can do to punish the partner. This is the set-up phase, because it sets up future abuse. The cycle of violence continues.

Substance Abuse

While substance abuse does not cause violence, it can trigger violent behavior in a violent person. Substance abuse is the misuse of legal drugs, such as alcohol or prescription medicine, and illegal drugs, such as methamphetamines or cocaine.

Alcohol, though, is the most used and abused drug in the United States. Every year, more than 14 million people in the United States abuse alcohol. Alcoholics tend to drink to numb painful feelings, release

---

Substance Abuse among Victims

The issues of substance abuse and domestic violence are connected for both the abuser and the victim. According to the NCADV, abused women are 15 times more likely to abuse alcohol and nine times more likely to abuse drugs than non-abused women.

Drugs and alcohol affect the way people behave.

stress, and feel more confident. Alcohol lowers a person's inhibitions and impulse control, causing a person to act before considering the consequences of the action. For this reason, alcohol is often a factor in cases of domestic abuse. According to the Marin Institute, two-thirds of intimate-partner violence victims reported that alcohol was involved. Approximately 480,000 children are mistreated each year by a caregiver with alcohol problems.

Perceptions of Alcohol and Drug Abuse

According to the 2007 National Crime Victimization Survey, approximately 26 percent of victims of violence believed their abusers were using drugs or alcohol.

Drugs also play a role in some cases of domestic violence. Among illegal drugs, amphetamines may lead to more impulsive actions and violence than others. Amphetamines cause alertness, excitability, and muscle tension. They also magnify a person's natural tendencies, so that an aggressive person becomes even more aggressive while on the drug.

While using a substance, abusers may more easily make the choice to act violently and the violence can escalate to a higher level than if the abuser were sober. Attacks become more brutal and frequent. The abuser does not think before grabbing a gun or a knife and might seriously hurt or even kill the victim. After a violent attack, the abuser might then blame the substance for his or her loss of control. The abuser may use the substance again to numb the feelings of guilt or shame, and the cycle continues.

Domestic Violence

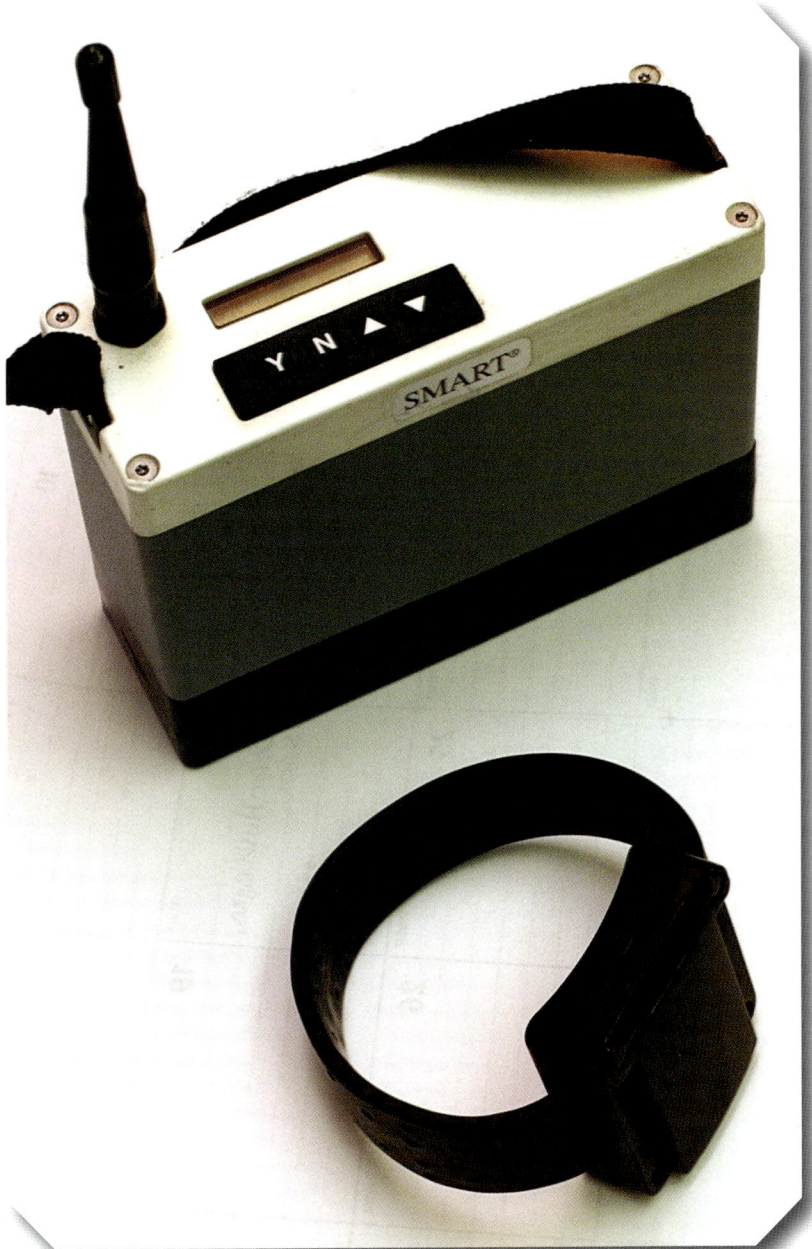

Even if convicted, some abusers return to attack their victims. Tracking devices help law enforcement monitor domestic violence offenders.

Chapter 5

Marchers hold silhouettes representing women who have died as a result of domestic violence.

Lasting Effects

Bruises and scars fade over time, but some of the effects of domestic violence never disappear. There can be long-term injuries that victims must live with for the rest of their lives. Sexual abuse can result in diseases that are incurable.

Emotional damage can cause a victim to consider suicide. And sometimes, victims turn to drugs or irresponsible behaviors to numb their emotions, keeping them from dealing with their traumatic pasts. Domestic violence has many lasting effects in the lives of children, intimate partners, and elders.

Health Consequences

Bruises, broken bones, and black eyes—these are common injuries that can result from physical abuse. The National Violence Against Women Survey found that approximately 552,000 women and 125,000 men seek medical attention each year for injuries resulting from domestic violence. Sometimes victims have injuries that require stitches. Victims can suffer from fractured skulls and vertebrae or be burned by acid or hot appliances. Abuse may also damage internal organs.

Some injuries heal, but others cause future health issues. For instance, a victim who suffers facial fractures might later experience recurring sinus infections. Victims can suffer from chronic pain and arthritis after repeated injuries and may also be at a higher risk of having asthma, diabetes, hypertension, and heart disease. Death is the most severe result

Battered Woman Syndrome

The term *battered woman syndrome* was first used by Dr. Lenore E. Walker to describe the mental and emotional state of a woman involved in an abusive relationship. A battered woman is someone who has been the victim of at least two cycles of violent behavior from an abuser. The characteristics of the syndrome are:
- The woman believes the violence is her fault.
- The woman is unable to blame another person for the violence.
- The woman fears for her own life and the lives of her children.
- The woman feels as if the abuser is constantly watching her and is aware of everything she does.

This syndrome has been used in court cases to explain the actions of abused women who used violence in their relationships, such as killing or injuring their abusers.

of physical violence. The NCADV reports that 16,800 homicides each year are due to intimate partner violence. Some murders are committed by the abuser, but the victims can also become murderers. After years of emotional, physical, and sexual violence, a victim can kill the abuser just to end the abuse.

Elders can suffer similar injuries, but they might be unable to go to a hospital or doctor to receive treatment. If neglected, elders can become unhealthy and die from starvation or dehydration. Similarly, children who are physically abused might not receive medical attention for their injuries. Untreated injuries can result in lasting health consequences. Because of their size, children are also at a high risk of death from physical abuse.

Sexual Issues

Sexual assault and rape happen often in many abusive relationships.

Domestic Violence

Forced sexual contact can harm the genital areas, causing infections, pain, or bleeding. If the abuser does not use protection, such as a condom, the victim is at risk of contracting sexually transmitted infections (STIs). These diseases include chlamydia, gonorrhea, syphilis, herpes, trichomoniasis, and human immunodeficiency virus (HIV). HIV can lead to acquired immunodeficiency syndrome (AIDS), which can cause a person's eventual death. According to the NCADV, women who are in violent relationships are three times more likely to get HIV/AIDS. Sometimes abusers intentionally infect their victims with STIs to keep them from having sex with others. Rape can also result in unplanned pregnancies, which can be an added stress to an abusive relationship.

Children who are sexually abused or who witness sexual abuse in the home can be severely traumatized.

"Surveys of females in the juvenile justice system and in shelters indicate rates of sexual abuse and assault of over 70 percent. The response of these girls is often to run away from home, which too frequently leads to engaging in prostitution."[1]
—P. Chamberlain & J. Reid,
in the Journal of Child and Family Studies

They may contract the same diseases as adults and suffer from damage to their genital areas. Children's bodies are not fully developed and children are not physically or emotionally ready to engage in sexual activity. Child victims may grow up believing that marital rape or incest are acceptable forms of behavior. This can put them at a higher risk of becoming abusers or victims as adults. The cycle of violence will then be passed from one generation to the next.

Emotional Trauma

Living with abuse can cause high amounts of stress. This emotional strain causes a variety of problems. Stress often leads to depression—a general feeling of hopelessness, lack of motivation, and a lack of energy. Depressed victims may feel they deserve to be abused or that there is no possible way to escape the abuse.

Violence during Pregnancy

Many abusers do not stop the abuse if their partner is pregnant. Abuse during pregnancy puts the unborn baby at risk of injury or even death through miscarriage. Pregnant women who experience domestic violence are more likely to delay their prenatal care, experience first- and second-trimester bleeding, have low weight gain, and suffer from infections.

Domestic Violence

Leslie Evans was abused by her husband. After she sought help, she showed symptoms related to post-traumatic stress disorder.

They are likely to entertain thoughts of suicide and may turn to drugs or alcohol in an attempt to cope with their emotional pain. Depression can also lead to physical problems, such as backaches, insomnia, and gastrointestinal issues.

Post-traumatic stress disorder (PTSD) is another form of emotional trauma that can result from domestic abuse. PTSD is a disorder that also affects soldiers, hostages, and prisoners of war. It lasts long after a traumatic event, such as a beating, and causes intense feelings of distress in victims. If reminded of the event, victims relive the moment, experiencing the same fear and anxiety as they did during the violence. PTSD can cause headaches, nightmares, fearfulness, and numbness. Victims often feel detached from others, have trouble concentrating, and may feel guilty for surviving the violence when others may not have survived or were more seriously injured. Children withdraw from activities in school, skip school, or may become overly aggressive with others.

Social Problems

When children suffering from PTSD or other domestic violence–related issues grow into adolescents, they may act out in unsafe ways. Some teenagers become impulsive and behave recklessly. They might skip school, commit crimes, or abuse drugs. Teenagers may also become involved in violent dating relationships. Some run away from their violent home environment to live on the streets, where they can become involved with criminal lifestyles such as drug dealing and prostitution.

If sexual abuse was part of the violence at home, teens are much more likely to enter into prostitution.

Domestic Violence

As a sex worker, a person is at risk of contracting STIs and of being abused by pimps and customers. Many times, a pimp starts out as the teen's boyfriend. The boyfriend is kind at first, but he later convinces the victim to enter into prostitution. Then, the boyfriend beats and threatens the victim who wants to stop being a prostitute. Adults can also be forced into prostitution by their abusers. It becomes one more way for an abuser to control the victim.

As drugs and crime affect communities, domestic violence becomes a noticeable social

Teen Dating Violence

Going out on dates and having a first boyfriend or girlfriend are normal parts of being a teenager. However, having a lack of experience in relationships and having witnessed violence at home can make a teenager susceptible to teen dating violence. Teens can mistake jealousy and possessiveness as signs of intense feelings of love. In reality, these are signs that violence could become part of the relationship.

Teen dating violence is very similar to domestic violence. One partner wants to control the other partner and uses emotional, physical, and sexual abuse to do so. A survey by the group Teenage Research Unlimited showed that "1 in 5 teens who have been in a serious relationship report being hit, slapped or pushed by a partner."[2] Teens might be reluctant to tell anyone about the abuse, though. They want to be independent from their parents and they might feel ashamed.

Digital abuse is also part of teen dating violence. According to the Family Violence Prevention Fund, "One in four teens in a relationship say they have been called names, harassed or put down by their partner through cellphones and texting."[3]

Essential Issues

issue, not just a hidden family issue. The abuse spreads into society, as juvenile detention centers and jails are filled with people who have been affected by domestic violence.

"I've had friends that have had problems, more mental than physical. Like the guy will try to brainwash her, make her think she's not going to be anything without him, or if he's not in her life, she won't have anybody. He won't let her think of any other person, she can't talk to or barely look at other guys or he'll get mad. Manipulating.... I tried to talk to my friend in this situation. She would just say it's not a big deal but she'd say, *We were fighting, messing around,* and she'd show me bruises. She laughs about it. She doesn't go out with us anymore, always with him...."[4]
—*A teen's story of abuse from Kati, age 15*

Domestic Violence

A student views a collection of artwork created by children and youth who have witnessed domestic violence.

Chapter 6

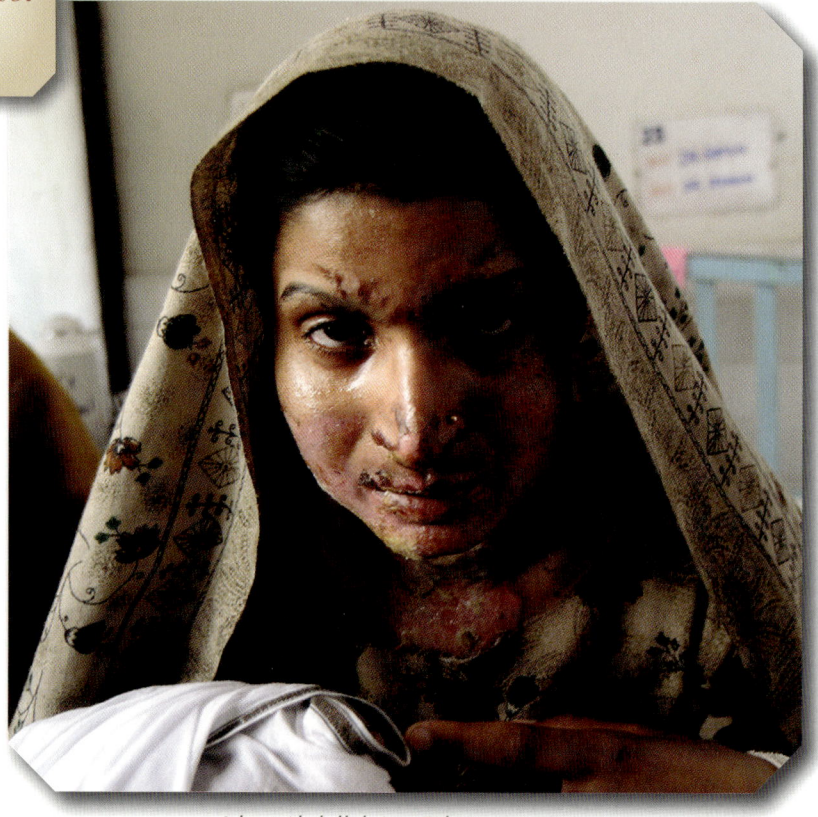

Ishrat Abdullah is a Pakistani woman whose husband threw sulfuric acid on her during a dispute in 2005.

A Global Issue

In the past 40 years, domestic violence has been acknowledged as a serious social problem in the United States. In some other cultures and countries around the world, though, domestic violence is still considered to be a private or family

Domestic Violence

matter, and cases of abuse are rarely investigated or punished. In some societies, where women are viewed as inferior to men, a man's right to beat or otherwise control women is upheld by law or even encouraged by religious or cultural tradition. From birth to old age, women in these cultures are abused or killed without protection from the law.

A 2005 study by the World Health Organization (WHO) found that more than 50 percent of the women in Bangladesh, Ethiopia, Peru, and Tanzania had been physically or sexually abused by an intimate partner. Child abuse is also a worldwide problem. According to the WHO, international studies have shown that "approximately 20% of women and 5–10% of men report being sexually abused as children, while 25–50% of all children report being physically abused."[1] In many places, domestic violence and child abuse are not talked about. These practices are tolerated and accepted, which allows the abuse to continue from one generation to the next.

Around the world, millions of domestic violence victims are physically, emotionally, and sexually abused each year. In addition to this abuse, there are several traditional practices that are forms of violence against women and children.

Essential Issues

> "Violence against women is a manifestation of historically unequal power relations between men and women, which have led to domination over and discrimination against women by men and to the prevention of the full advancement of women. . . ."[2]
>
> —The United Nations Declaration on the Elimination of Violence Against Women, *December 1993*

The Missing Millions

Some cultures value sons over daughters, and in these cultures the practice of selective abortion or infanticide has prevented or ended the lives of millions of girls. Infanticide is the killing of children shortly after their birth. In India, there are nearly 10,000 cases of female infanticide each year. China promotes a one-child policy that limits couples to having one child throughout their lifetimes. In a survey there, it was found that 12 percent of female embryos are aborted or somehow lost. And when girls are born, they may be deprived of proper nutrition or health care, causing death or mental and physical disabilities. An estimated 60 million women are "missing" from population statistics because of these practices, meaning that the actual number of females in the country is significantly less than it should predictably be. Sex-selective abortion, female infanticide, and differing nutritional and health care access for female children is mostly found in South Asia, North Africa, the Middle East, and China.

Early Marriage

In some countries, particularly in South Asia and Africa, girls younger than 15 are forced into early marriages. Poverty-stricken families often marry off their daughters to reduce their financial burden. Many girls are wed shortly after puberty and most do not have a say in their futures. The girls are then limited in their ability to pursue their independence and education. Early marriages can also adversely affect a girl's health, because bearing children before the body is fully mature can be damaging.

> "My husband slaps me, has sex with me against my will and I have to conform. Before being interviewed I didn't really think about this. I thought this is only natural. This is the way a husband behaves."[3]
> —Woman interviewed in Bangladesh, from a WHO study

Forced Prostitution

Another way desperately poor families survive is by selling their daughters into prostitution. This may

Essential Issues

Reasons for Beating

Women who participated in the WHO Multi-Country Study on Women's Health and Domestic Violence were asked if certain reasons justified wife beating. These reasons included the wife not completing housework, refusing to have sex, disobedience, and unfaithfulness. The reason most often believed to justify female beating was unfaithfulness, followed by disobedience. However, many women responded with a belief that no circumstances justify wife beating. The majority of women responding this way lived in urban settings.

not be done intentionally; in many cases the girls are sent to work as domestic servants and are physically or sexually abused by their employers or are forced into prostitution without the family's knowledge. In some parts of the world, however, such as poor, rural areas of Thailand, it is believed to be the daughter's duty to prostitute herself in order to help her poverty-stricken family. In Northern Ghana, parts of Togo, and southern India, girls are sometimes "donated" to shrines and temples to be sexual servants to priests. In turn, the families receive religious protection.

Bride Burning

In India, more than 5,000 women are killed each year over disputes related to dowries, or bride prices. According to tradition, the groom receives a dowry from the bride's family, which might include large sums of money, farm animals, furniture, or electronics. If the husband's dowry demands are not met before and after marriage, the husband or his family might kill the bride, often by setting her on fire. The incident is reported as death by "accidental" fire or suicide. An estimated five women are burned to death daily in India and four women daily in Pakistan in issues relating to domestic disputes. While the dowry practice is illegal, it is still common and the killings continue.

Honor Killings

In some countries, particularly in traditionally Islamic nations in the Middle East and North Africa, women may be killed to protect the family honor. Several things are regarded

Female Genital Mutilation

Female genital mutilation (FGM) is a cutting ritual performed on some girls and women. FGM is a practice with deep traditional roots in Africa and some parts of the Middle East. It is usually part of a fertility or coming-of-age ceremony that is thought to ensure chastity, and it is performed on females between infancy and age 15. The procedure involves cutting or removing parts of the female genitalia and sometimes partially sealing the vaginal opening. Approximately 100 to 140 million women have undergone the procedure, with 92 million being from Africa. Each year, 3 million girls are at risk of FGM.

The consequences of FGM are painful and sometimes life threatening. Immediately after the procedure, complications can include severe bleeding and pain, bacterial infections, and urine retention. The long-term consequences include recurrent bladder infections, cysts, infertility, higher risk of childbirth complications and infant deaths, and the need for later surgeries to repair the damage or allow for childbirth.

Essential Issues

as disgracing a family's honor, including being a rape victim, committing adultery, having premarital relationships, and falling in love with a person of whom the family disapproves. Typically, fathers or brothers kill the women accused of dishonor. It is estimated that 5,000 women are killed each year in these so-called honor killings.

Immigrant Communities

As immigrants move to the United States and other countries, some bring their beliefs about domestic violence into their new communities. They may continue their traditional practices, such as honor killings or female genital mutilation, even when these practices are illegal in their adopted country. They also might practice physical, emotional, or sexual abuse in their families.

In the United States, domestic violence happens in all communities

Honor Killings in the United States

Several murders described as honor killings have occurred in the United States. One of these occurred on October 20, 2009, in Arizona. Noor Almaleki, a 20-year-old woman from Iraq, was fatally injured when her father ran her down with his car. Her father, Faleh Almaleki, was determined to kill her because he believed Almaleki had brought shame onto their family by becoming too "Westernized."

Another honor killing occurred in 2008 in Texas when Yaser Said shot and killed his two teenage girls, Sarah and Amina. He was upset because they were dating non-Muslim boys. Said had a history of physically abusing his wife and daughters and has since disappeared, evading prosecution.

Domestic Violence

Amina and Sarah Said were victims of an honor killing. Their photo is featured on an ad campaign aimed to raise awareness about honor killings.

and is a criminal act punishable by law. However, several factors can keep immigrant abuse victims from seeking or receiving assistance. For one thing, many immigrants are initially unaware of the laws protecting them and the services available to

Essential Issues

help them. There might also be language barriers preventing them from reaching out for help. Away from their families and friends and in a new, foreign place, an immigrant victim can feel isolated and helpless. In addition, because of their immigration status, victims may not be able to obtain work that would allow them to be financially independent from their abusive spouses, so they may feel they have no choice but to stay in the relationship. Abusers may even threaten to have them deported if they tell anyone about the abuse.

Domestic Violence

A mock funeral in Israel in 2010 was created to draw attention to the growing number of women killed due to domestic violence in that country.

Chapter 7

Washington State law enforcement officer Kent Mundell was fatally shot on December 21, 2009, while responding to a domestic violence call.

Law Enforcement and the Legal System

When an act of domestic violence occurs, law enforcement and the legal system may become involved. This usually happens when an emergency 911 call is made, often by a victim, a neighbor, or a child in the home. Once

Domestic Violence

the dispatcher hears that domestic violence may be the problem, police officers are sent to the home.

If the call is coming from inside the home, the dispatcher tries to keep the caller on the line until officers arrive. A dispatcher will find out if the violence is physical or verbal, whether there are injuries, and if weapons are involved. It is also important for law enforcement to know whether the suspect is intoxicated, whether there are protection orders against the suspect, and who else is in the home. The dispatcher updates the officers and keeps the caller aware of the time the officers will arrive.

The next step in the response process is made by law enforcement. Police are cautious when entering a domestic violence scene—they know emotions are high and weapons or substance abuse might be involved. Many times the police have been to

Assessing a Violent Situation

Erin H. House, the legal advocacy coordinator for the Domestic Violence Project/SAFE House, recommends the following considerations for police officers when assessing a violent situation:

- Find out exactly what happened by getting a clear description of the event. A batterer will usually lie about the situation and not offer a clear description or be uninterested in giving a description. Victims will likely want to tell their stories to officers.
- Victims may take responsibility for the abuse, saying that it was somehow their fault. Abusers will blame the victims and talk about the bad qualities of the victims.
- Think carefully about the injuries inflicted. Are they offensive or defensive? Scratches on the face or bite marks on the arms are usually signs of defensive wounds.

the home on a previous call. Police must first look for and gain control of any weapons. Then, they separate the people involved in the violence and keep them out of hearing distance from each other. Police assess the victim and suspect for injuries and obtain accounts of the incident from both parties. Police also interview witnesses to the assault. If medical treatment is needed, police call for emergency medical services. Then, according to state laws, the officers usually make an arrest.

Arrest Policies

Most states have mandatory arrest policies, but some states leave the arrest decision up to the officer. Mandatory arrest policies require police officers to arrest a suspect if they believe an assault has occurred. Arrests must be made, even if the victim does not want the abuser to be arrested. Mandatory arrests in domestic violence cases became widely practiced in the mid-1980s after an experimental study was conducted in Minneapolis, Minnesota. The study concluded that arrest deterred violence more successfully than any other action. After the results of the study were published, the US attorney general recommended that mandatory arrest become

Domestic Violence

the standard police response to domestic violence. Many states then adopted a mandatory or pro-arrest policy for domestic violence calls.

Debates exist on whether automatically arresting abusers is effective in stopping the abuse. Some studies affirmed the findings of the Minneapolis experiment, but others contradicted the results. Mandatory arrest may have been best in the Minneapolis community, but in other communities, it did not seem to be the best solution. Some experts in

The Minneapolis Domestic Violence Experiment

In early 1980, an experiment was conducted in Minneapolis, Minnesota, to determine how police could most effectively deal with domestic violence cases. At the time, there were three common ways to handle cases of domestic abuse. The traditional approach involved the police asking the abuser to leave the home to cool off. The second approach, recommended by psychologists, was to mediate the argument that had preceded the violence. Mediation is when a third party—in this case, the police officer—discusses the argument with the two parties involved in order to help them come to an agreeable resolution. The third approach was to treat the violence as a crime and to make an arrest.

The Minneapolis experiment randomly assigned domestic violence cases to arrest or another police response. Police were given pads of color-coded report forms. Each color stood for a different response to a domestic violence call. The officers responded to each call according to the color of the report form at the top of the pad. After the results of the Minneapolis experiment were analyzed, it was found that arresting abusers reduced the odds of repeat violence by 50 percent.

Essential Issues

Debra Laberdie is a 911 dispatcher who has answered calls relating to domestic abuse. She has also dealt with domestic violence in her own life.

law enforcement believe that arresting the alleged abuser without considering the specific situation can sometimes do more harm than good. Others believe that taking the guesswork out of handling domestic violence calls ensures that the victim will always be protected. If an immediate arrest is made, the victim is immediately separated from the violence and is given time to leave the home safely.

Dual Arrests

When making an arrest, police first need to identify who is the abuser and who is the victim. Sometimes this can be difficult to determine. A victim may fight back and injure the abuser. Both parties are upset and arguing—is it the man or the woman who is the victim? Same-sex relationships present a unique situation, because the stereotypical gender roles do not apply. For all of these reasons, officers may not be able to tell which person is most at fault. They then will decide to make a dual arrest.

Arrest Survey

In 2008, the National Institute of Justice conducted a survey about domestic violence arrests. Some of the findings included the following:

• Arrest rates increased if a minor was present.

• Arrest rates increased if a victim was injured.

• Men were twice as likely as women to reoffend.

Essential Issues

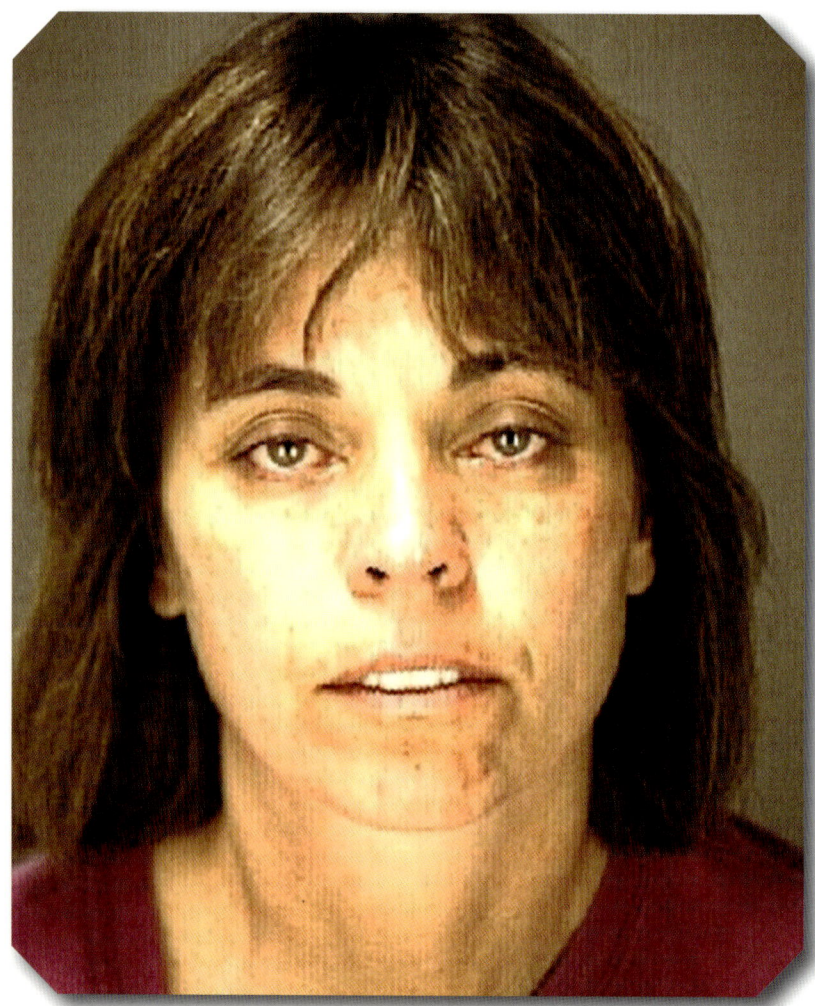

Stephanie Studebaker and her husband were both charged with domestic violence when law enforcement responded to a disturbance at their home.

A dual arrest is made when the police determine that mutual battering is involved. There are issues with making dual arrests, though. Many times

Domestic Violence

batterers inflict injuries that are not easily visible, while a victim will inflict injuries anywhere while reacting to the abuse. This can make it appear that the victim is the abuser, because the injuries inflicted are easier to see. That is why it is important for officers to look at the past criminal histories of the parties involved instead of only looking at the current situation.

Protection Orders

If victims wish to take legal action against their abusers, they may obtain civil protection orders, also known as restraining orders. A protection order prohibits an abuser from making physical and verbal contact with his or her victim. The order usually provides rules for child custody and visitation, evicts the abuser from the home, requires the abuser to undergo counseling or participate in a batterer or

Filing a Protection Order

Each state has different rules for filing a protection order, and some of the rules can cause difficulties for victims. Some states charge a filing fee and court costs, while other states do not charge anything. Victims may also need to pay a lawyer's fees. These can be major obstacles to victims. Weeks might pass before victims receive their protection orders from the courts.

The legal system can be complicated, but abuse victims have public resources to help them. Local domestic violence shelters and hotlines are available to help victims through the legal process.

substance abuse treatment program, and restricts gun possession. If the abuser violates the protection order, he or she may be tried in court and receive fines or jail time as punishment.

The problem with protection orders is that they are difficult to enforce. Nearly 60 percent of protection orders are violated within the first year; however, officers cannot make an arrest unless they either personally witness a violation or obtain a warrant, a legal document issued by a court. In recent years, however, many state laws have changed to allow officers to make warrantless arrests for protection order violations.

The problem of domestic violence will never disappear. But fortunately, in the United States, victims of domestic violence have recourse to legal protection and are able to take steps to ensure their safety.

Domestic Violence

Law enforcement officers investigated a domestic violence scene in which a husband and wife were killed, and their daughter was injured.

Chapter 8

Mary Kay cosmetics consultants gathered at the US Capitol in 2005 to show their support for legislation offering help to victims of domestic violence.

Advocacy and Legislation

From the mid-1970s to today, domestic violence has become a highly recognized problem in the United States. Advocacy led to public awareness of the issue. Public awareness then led to legislation that protects the rights of victims. The

Domestic Violence

process has been evolutionary and is still developing. It began on a local level and grew to occupy a national platform.

Before the mid-1970s, victims of domestic violence often had nowhere to go when they left their abusers. There were few shelters, and law enforcement officers were trained to stay out of domestic violence situations. Between the mid-1970s and mid-1980s, advocates began opening shelters and providing services to battered women. There were few governmental services to help victims, so the shelters mostly provided a safe place for victims to rest for a few days. Realizing that victims needed more assistance, advocates approached legislators to create laws and public policies to meet the needs of the victims. Advocates also reached out within their communities and gathered support from businesses, organizations, churches, and private citizens. Shelters and services grew from community support.

Advocates work on behalf of victims. They speak out and act for justice. An advocate can work one-

Celebrity Advocates

Celebrities including actress Salma Hayek and singer Martina McBride have joined the fight against domestic violence by becoming spokespeople for the National Domestic Violence Hotline. Using their celebrity status, they publicly promote healthy relationships and educate people about domestic abuse.

on-one with victims to help them work with the legal system or receive certain benefits. An advocate can also work with community programs to change policies and procedures so that they will better help victims.

Landmark Case

Several landmark cases in the United States have made the public aware of the issue of domestic violence. In one such case, *Thurman v. City of Torrington* (1985), an abuse victim named Tracey Thurman sued the city of Torrington, Connecticut, alleging that city police had failed to immediately respond to her emergency call for help. Thurman made the call on June 10, 1983, about 15 minutes before her husband attacked her. By the time police arrived 25 minutes later, Thurman's husband had stabbed her in the chest, neck, and throat. When police arrived on the scene, they failed to arrest Mr. Thurman immediately, and instead watched while Mr. Thurman kicked his wife in the head twice.

Mrs. Thurman had been to the police station many times in the year prior to the stabbing, as her husband had repeatedly violated a legal order to stay away from her. She had attempted, without success, to have her husband arrested for his violations. The court ruled in favor of Mrs. Thurman, finding that she had been denied equal protection under the law, and Mrs. Thurman was awarded $2.3 million. The suit changed how officers in the city responded to domestic violence calls.

NATIONAL RECOGNITION

Until the mid-1980s, advocates working to provide services for domestic violence victims lacked federal funding to support their cause. In 1984, the issue became nationally recognized when the US surgeon general created a task force dedicated to combating family violence. Hearings were held on the issue and a report was released that outlined the magnitude of the problem.

In the report, recommendations were made for victim assistance, prevention and awareness, education and training, data collection and reporting, research, and legislative action. Some specific recommendations included the creation of a national public awareness campaign and 24-hour, toll-free hotlines. The report described the devastating effects of domestic abuse, stating:

> *To be abused by a spouse, a parent, a trusted adult or by one's own child or to witness such abuse, carries with it a particular agony. Victims wrestle with feelings of fear, loyalty, love, guilt and shame. In this they often face conflicts not experienced by those attacked by strangers. Adults will be torn between the desire to shield and help a loved one and their responsibility toward their own safety or others in the household. Children often face alone the terrible truth that those who should protect them are, in fact, a source of harm. Anyone who lives in a violent home experiences an essential loss. The one place on earth where they should feel safe and secure has become instead a place of danger.*[1]

Legislation against Domestic Abuse

The surgeon general's report was significant in bringing national attention to the issue of domestic violence in the United States. Later that same year, 1984, two important pieces of legislation were passed that directly affected the needs of victims: the Family Violence Prevention and Services Act (FVPSA) and the Victims of Crime Act (VOCA).

The FVPSA is the only federal funding source for domestic violence shelters and programs. While the bill expired in 2008, it was reauthorized in 2010 under the Child Abuse Prevention and Treatment Act (CAPTA), which addresses child abuse and neglect. The FVPSA helps millions of children and adults each year by providing funds for emergency shelters, crisis hotlines, counseling, legal assistance, safety planning, and preventative education. The act provides grants for local agencies and funds the National Domestic Violence Hotline.

The VOCA provides federal support to state and local agencies that assist victims of all types of crime. All VOCA funds come from fines and penalties paid by offenders. The funds pay victims directly by compensating them for out-of-pocket expenses. The money also funds victim assistance programs, such as domestic violence shelters and rape crisis centers. While VOCA funds help victims of many types of crimes, the money is especially important to domestic violence shelters and resource centers. According to a 2008 survey by the National Center for Victims of Crime, 99.5 percent of domestic violence service providers said that VOCA funds are very important to their operation. With funding from the FVPSA and VOCA, domestic violence shelters and resource providers have been able to help more victims and have a presence in every part of the country.

Violence Against Women Act

Advocates continued to work with legislators. In the early 1990s, the highly publicized O. J. Simpson trial brought increased national awareness to the issue of domestic violence. In 1994, the Violence Against Women

The O. J. Simpson Trial

On June 12, 1994, a high-profile murder case gripped the US public and brought the issue of domestic violence into the public eye. The victims were Nicole Brown Simpson and Ronald Goldman, who were found brutally stabbed to death in Los Angeles, California. Nicole's ex-husband, actor and former professional football star O. J. Simpson, was tried for the murders. During the nine-month trial, it came to light that there had been a history of domestic abuse in the marriage and that Simpson had made threats on Nicole's life. However, despite considerable evidence against him, Simpson was found not guilty of the two counts of murder.

O. J. Simpson was tried for the murder of his wife and her friend in 1994.

Act (VAWA) passed and was the first US federal legislation that acknowledged domestic violence and sexual assaults as being crimes. It also provided resources to help community-coordinated responses to domestic violence. VAWA was reauthorized in 2000 and again in 2005. Some of its provisions include grants that encourage arrest and enforce protection orders, provide housing opportunities for battered women, and help combat cyberstalking. The 2005 version added additional provisions, including funding for rape crisis centers, culturally specific services, and services for children and teenagers.

For some battered immigrant women, VAWA offers certain protections and a route to becoming legal residents of the United States. These women must be married to or recently divorced from US citizens or lawful residents. VAWA allows these battered women, along with their children, to petition for legal residency through several methods regardless of how they entered the

I-VAWA

I-VAWA is the International Violence Against Women Act. It was introduced in 2010 to use US programs and leadership to prevent violence worldwide, support survivors, and hold abusers accountable. While this legislation has not yet been enacted, it did pass a Senate committee vote in December 2010.

Senator John Kerry, who introduced the bill, said, "This bill tells women and girls that they are valued, respected members of society who do not have to suffer in silence. I-VAWA will use U.S. assistance wisely, bring greater transparency, and improve coordination inside the government and with key stakeholders in civil society. But more importantly, we are saying that now is the time for us to gather the resources and political will to turn *I-VAWA's* promise into a reality for the millions of women and girls whose lives will be improved as a result of this critical legislation."[2]

Essential Issues

country and without informing their spouses. If battered women can gain independence from their abusers, they have a better chance of leaving abusive marriages and being able to support themselves.

National legislation and funding keep afloat vital services for victims of domestic violence. In cities and rural communities across the nation, these services help millions of people each year. Shelters, hotlines, and other programs not only save lives, but also provide victims and abusers with resources to help end the cycle of abuse.

Asylum in the United States

Women who believe they are at risk of female genital mutilation (FGM) may seek asylum in the United States. Asylum is protection offered to an immigrant who faces danger in his or her homeland. The protection offered is permanent residency. FGM is considered a form of persecution by the US government.

Domestic Violence

In 2005, actress Salma Hayek testified on behalf of reauthorizing the Violence Against Women Act at a Senate committee meeting.

Chapter 9

Actresses perform in a high school play highlighting issues of domestic and dating abuse. Television, film, and theater can educate the public about the subject.

Breaking the Cycle

If a victim makes the decision to leave an abusive relationship, he or she will need the help of friends, family, and the community. Receiving immediate help and a safe place to hide is what many victims initially need. After that first

Domestic Violence

step out of their violent situation, victims may take advantage of community resources such as emergency shelters, free counseling, and parenting classes. Many communities offer rehabilitation and counseling services for batterers, as well, and seek to educate the public to prevent future violence.

Hotlines

As the first step in breaking the cycle of violence, a victim or a family member might call a hotline for help. National and local hotlines are available 24 hours a day and many have both English- and Spanish-speaking advocates who answer calls. Callers remain anonymous while receiving vital information. Advocates assist callers by providing crisis intervention, information, and referrals.

Crisis intervention helps callers understand and identify the problems they are experiencing and the possible solutions. The intervention also helps callers create safety plans. Callers are told about resources that can help them. Callers can learn about intervention

National Domestic Violence Hotline

As part of VAWA, the National Domestic Violence Hotline was established in 1996. It has access to more than 4,000 domestic violence shelters and programs in the United States, Puerto Rico, and the US Virgin Islands. The hotline offers intervention and referrals to victims, abusers, advocates, friends, and families.

Vice President Joe Biden visited the National Domestic Violence Hotline Center in Texas in 2009.

programs for batterers and also receive guidance through the criminal justice system. Advocates give callers referrals to shelters and programs, social-service agencies, legal programs, and other organizations dedicated to the issue.

Hotlines are a critical connection to help for victims. In a 2009 survey, which occurred in a 24-hour period across the country, the National

Domestic Violence

Network to End Domestic Violence (NNEDV) found that domestic violence programs answered more than 960 hotline calls every hour. In that period, the survey found that 23,045 total hotline calls were answered across the United States.

Shelters

If callers are in immediate danger and need a safe place to go, advocates refer them to shelters in their communities. Shelters are buildings or apartments where victims and their children can stay for a night, a few days, or even a few weeks. Basic needs are met in the shelter, including food and clothing. Shelters are emergency housing, and are not meant to be long-term residences. In the NNEDV survey, it was found that more than 21,000 people across the United States were housed at emergency shelter services over a 24-hour period. Most shelters are

The First Women's Shelter

Women's Advocates in St. Paul, Minnesota, was the first shelter in the United States for battered women and their children. It was founded in 1974 and began as a crisis line, which women could call to receive legal information and advice. The advocates realized that victims needed to go to a safe, physical space to escape the violence at home. After reaching out to the community, Women's Advocates received the needed donations to purchase a house to build their shelter.

Today, the shelter has 15 bedrooms and six community bathrooms, which enable Women's Advocates to serve 45 women and children each day. At the shelter, residents have their basic needs met and also receive counseling and support. Women's Advocates, which has been open for more than 30 years, serves approximately 1,000 women and children each year.

only for women and children, but some accept men as well.

While in a shelter, victims may join support groups for people who have experienced domestic violence. In the groups, victims share their stories. They learn that they are not alone and that domestic violence is a widespread problem. This is especially important to victims, as many have become isolated while in their abusive relationships. Victims may also receive individual counseling from therapists.

As shelters only provide temporary housing, advocates help victims find transitional housing, a type of shelter where victims may stay for longer periods of time. They also connect victims with employment programs and with educational opportunities that can put them on the path toward living independently. These programs and services empower victims to remain free of their abusive relationships and to survive on their own.

Children's Needs

Attending to the needs of children in the shelters is also an important part of intervention. Children in abusive families are in a stressful situation and may not have the communication skills necessary to

Domestic Violence

deal with their emotions. For this reason, group counseling sessions can be especially valuable for children. Tools used to help children include role-playing, discussions, and art projects. Shelters frequently offer parenting classes to adults to help them become more effective parents. An adult who grew up in a violent home most likely had poor parenting role models.

> "A young woman with a 2-day-old baby called today requesting shelter. She didn't want to go home because her abuser had beaten her just before she went into labor."[1]
> —Missouri advocate, from the Domestic Violence Counts 2009 *census*

Advocates at a shelter will also work with a child to create a safety plan. If the family returns to the violent situation, having a safety plan will help the child. Shelters may also provide school services to keep children from falling behind with their educations.

Rehabilitation Programs

Many community organizations offer classes to teach batterers about the effects of domestic violence with the ultimate goal of eliminating relationship violence. The courts may require some offenders to attend these programs, but others attend voluntarily. In some programs, batterers are not allowed to contact victims. Typical batterer intervention programs emphasize critical thinking skills, conflict resolution skills, and group therapy sessions. Batterers learn about honesty, sexual respect, and negotiation and fairness. Longer-term batterer programs, those lasting for more than 12 months, typically include programs and discussion about childhood shame, power and control, and gender equality. Many programs deal with substance abuse issues as well, so part of the intervention helps the person get "clean" and sober. Programs exist for heterosexual or homosexual men and women.

Not everyone believes that

Batterer Treatment Programs

Beginning in the mid to late 1970s, programs for batterers began developing. Some of the first recognized programs were the Emerge program (in Boston, Massachusetts), RAVEN (in St. Louis, Missouri), Alternatives to Aggression (in Madison, Wisconsin), and psychologist Anne Ganley's batterer program (in Tacoma, Washington).

While not the first batterer program in the United States, the Duluth Model of Treatment was created and used in the city of Duluth, Minnesota, in the early 1980s. A unique feature of the Duluth model is that it utilizes numerous community agencies, from police officers to probation officers, to provide a coordinated and consistent effort to stop domestic violence. The curriculum created for the Duluth Model focuses on issues of power and control, which typically drive violence in abusive relationships. It also differentiates between cases involving physical battering and those that do not. It has since become a model of treatment and community coordination used by domestic violence programs and treatment centers throughout the world. Over the last 30 years, programs for domestic violence abusers have grown from just a few to the point where there are now literally hundreds of treatment programs for domestic violence batterers throughout the United States.

batterer intervention programs are effective, however. Success in the programs is difficult to define. Does success mean a complete elimination of abuse, or a reduction in abuse? While a batterer might stop the physical abuse, the emotional or psychological abuse could worsen. Some believe the programs only work for a short period of time, and that batterers soon return to their violent behavior. And if a batterer does reduce the frequency of violent episodes, any violence is still harmful to a victim. According to a report by the National Institute of Justice,

> *The field of batterer intervention is still in its infancy, and much remains to be learned. . . . As [batterer intervention programs] are a relatively new response to a critical social problem, it is too early to abandon the concept. It is also too early to believe that we have all the answers.*[2]

Prevention

Since domestic violence is a learned behavior, spreading the message about its effects is vital to ending the cycle. Most domestic violence programs have educational outreach programs to inform the public, police officers, teachers, and health-care workers about the signs and effects of

Essential Issues

Start Strong

Targeted at 11- to 14-year-olds, Start Strong is a program that educates teens about healthy relationships and the prevention of teen dating violence. The program, which can be found in cities throughout the United States, uses innovative ways to reach teens. Some programs use music and social media to engage youth. The program in Rhode Island created a three-dimensional video game called *Healthy Teens* to teach teens about healthy relationships. The programs work in classrooms to educate students and also team with educators, parents, and other organizations to bring awareness about teen dating violence.

domestic violence. National and local organizations use all types of media—from advertising campaigns to interactive Web sites for teens—to teach the difference between healthy and abusive relationships. Events in communities, such as candlelight vigils for murdered victims and national training conferences, bring more awareness about the issue.

Education is empowerment. It enables children and teens to make healthy decisions before starting a relationship. And adults and elders are empowered to escape relationships they are afraid to leave. Young people who are being abused or know someone who is should get help immediately by talking to a trusted adult, such as a parent, coach, counselor, or teacher. By bringing the secret out from behind closed doors, more families are protected, making it possible for the cycle of domestic violence to be broken.

Domestic Violence

Those who work on behalf of domestic violence victims continue to educate, advocate, and increase awareness of the issue.

Essential Issues

Timeline

600 BCE –400 CE
In ancient Rome, husbands have the legal right to beat or kill their wives and children.

400 CE –1400 CE
Medieval laws and the church encourage men to use violence to force women to obey their commands.

1792
British writer Mary Wollstonecraft writes one of the first books advocating for women's rights.

1970s
The battered women's movement begins and gains momentum throughout the decade.

1974
Women's Advocates in St. Paul, Minnesota, opens a shelter for battered women and children.

Domestic Violence

1869

John Stuart Mill publishes his book *The Subjection of Women*, which calls for an end to wife abuse.

1878

Frances Power Cobbe publishes her pamphlet "Wife Torture in England," which examines 6,000 cases of domestic violence.

1878

The Matrimonial Causes Act is passed into English law.

1980s

The Duluth Model of Treatment is created, emphasizing a coordinated community response to domestic violence.

1980

The Minneapolis Domestic Violence Experiment tests the best way for law enforcement to handle domestic violence calls.

1981

The first Day of Unity is held on October 1 in an effort to inform the community about domestic violence.

Timeline

1984
The US surgeon general releases a report on the domestic violence problem in the United States.

1984
Congress authorizes the Family Violence Prevention and Services Act.

1984
Congress authorizes the Victims of Crime Act.

1994
The Violence Against Women Act is authorized by Congress. It is reauthorized in 2000 and 2005.

1996
The National Domestic Violence Hotline is established.

2007
On June 9, Ambrosio Analco injures his daughter and kills his ex-girlfriend Nicole McAffee, their twin sons, two other adults, and himself.

Domestic Violence

1987
The first observation of Domestic Violence Awareness Month takes place.

1994
O. J. Simpson is tried for the murders of his wife and her friend, bringing national attention to the issue of domestic violence. He is found not guilty.

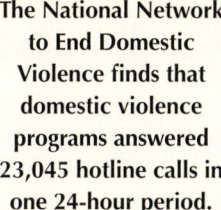

1994
The "Remember My Name" project, a national registry of women killed by an intimate partner, is started in October.

2008
Yaser Said kills his two daughters, Sarah and Amina, in an honor killing in Texas.

2009
The National Network to End Domestic Violence finds that domestic violence programs answered 23,045 hotline calls in one 24-hour period.

2010
The Family Violence Prevention and Services Act is reauthorized under the Child Abuse Prevention and Treatment Act.

Essential Issues

Essential Facts

At Issue

❖ Globally, domestic violence is a widespread problem. The violence not only affects victims but also family members who witness the violence. Intimate partners, elders, and children can be victims of abuse.

❖ The effects of domestic violence can be both short- and long-term. Health consequences from physical abuse include broken bones and internal injuries. Sexual abuse can result in sexually transmitted infections and bodily damage. And emotional trauma can lead to depression and thoughts of suicide. In some cases, the abuse results in death.

❖ Social problems result from domestic violence. Teens and adults run away from home and can become homeless. While on the streets, victims may become involved in prostitution or drug abuse.

❖ Teen dating violence is a growing problem. Teens who witness violence at home are likely to become involved in abusive relationships.

❖ In some cultures, traditional practices are forms of violence against women. These practices include sex-selective abortion or infanticide, early marriages, forced prostitution, female genital mutilation, bride burning, and honor killings. Immigrant communities may bring harmful traditional practices to their new countries.

❖ Most law enforcement agencies have mandatory arrest policies for domestic violence calls. But some believe these policies do not stop abuse and, in some cases, may do more harm than good.

❖ Many services have been created to help victims in abusive relationships. Intervention programs exist to help abusers become less violent. Some, however, question whether batterer intervention programs can eliminate abuse.

Domestic Violence

Critical Dates

1974
Those working to stop domestic abuse realized that battered women and their children need a safe physical space to escape abuse. Women's Advocates, the first shelter for battered women and children, was opened in St. Paul, Minnesota.

1980s
Awareness about the issue of domestic abuse increased after the US surgeon general released a report on the domestic violence problem in the United States. Congress authorized numerous acts related to the issue, including the Family Violence Prevention and Services Act and the Victims of Crime Act.

1980
The Minneapolis Domestic Violence Experiment tested the best way for law enforcement to handle domestic violence calls. After this experiment, many law enforcement agencies in the country adopted mandatory arrest policies for domestic violence calls.

1996
Another resource for victims was created when the National Domestic Violence Hotline was established.

Quotes

"Domestic violence causes far more pain than the visible marks of bruises and scars. It is devastating to be abused by someone that you love and think loves you in return. It is estimated that approximately 3 million incidents of domestic violence are reported each year in the United States. Tragically, domestic violence remains a pervasive threat to the fabric of America's families and the well-being of America's future."—*US Senator Dianne Feinstein, in her October 6, 2004, statement to the 108th Congress on Domestic Violence in America*

Glossary

advocacy
   The act of supporting a cause.

batterer
   Someone who engages in a pattern of coercively controlling behavior including physical, verbal, emotional, and sexual abuse.

chastity
   The state of being pure, modest, and innocent of unlawful sexual intercourse.

depression
   An emotional disorder that includes sadness, inactivity, feelings of hopelessness, and sometimes, suicidal tendencies.

dispatcher
   A person who answers emergency calls and sends law enforcement or emergency medical services to the scene of an accident or a crime.

hypertension
   High blood pressure.

insomnia
   The abnormal inability to sleep.

intervention
   An effort to stop a harmful action from occurring.

legislation
   Rules or laws.

mandatory
   Containing a command; obligatory.

marital rape
   Forcing a spouse to have sexual intercourse against his or her will.

prostitution
   The act of engaging in sexual relations for money.

puberty
   A time when a person's body matures into becoming capable of sexual reproduction.

sex-selective abortion
   An abortion that is performed to remove a fetus of a particular sex.

stalking
   To pursue obsessively and harass.

stereotypical
   Something that conforms to a common or assumed pattern.

subservient
   Inferior or submissive.

syndrome
   A group of symptoms that characterize a particular condition.

victimization
   To make a victim of someone.

Additional Resources

Selected Bibliography

"The Facts on Teen Dating and Violence." *endabuse.org*. The Family Violence Prevention Fund, 2009. Web.

Sherman, Lawrence W. *Policing Domestic Violence*. New York: The Free Press, 1992. Print.

Webb, M. *Domestic Abuse: Our Stories*. Baltimore, MD: Publish America, 2004. Print.

Wilson, K. J. *When Violence Begins at Home*. Alameda, CA: Hunter House, 2006. Print.

Further Readings

Dziedzic, Nancy, ed. *Family Violence*. Farmington Hills, MI: Greenhaven Press, 2009. Print.

Kittleson, Mark J., ed. *The Truth About Abuse*. New York: Facts On File, 2005. Print.

Moles, Kerry. *The Teen Relationship Workbook: For Professionals Helping Teens to Develop Healthy Relationships and Prevent Domestic Violence*. Beachwood, OH: Wellness Reproductions & Publishing, 2001.

Web Links

To learn more about domestic violence, visit ABDO Publishing Company online at **www.abdopublishing.com**. Web sites about domestic violence are featured on our Book Links page. These links are routinely monitored and updated to provide the most current information available.

Domestic Violence

For More Information

For more information on this subject, contact or visit the following organizations:

National Coalition Against Domestic Violence
1120 Lincoln Street, Suite #1603, Denver, CO 80203
303-839-1852
www.ncadv.org
The National Coalition Against Domestic Violence works to make the issue of domestic violence a top political and legislative issue. Its mission is to end domestic violence, empower battered women and children, promote and unify direct service providers, alert and educate the public, and promote partnerships.

The National Domestic Violence Hotline
PO Box 161810, Austin, TX 78716
512-794-1133
800-799-SAFE(7233) or TTY 800-787-3224
www.thehotline.org
Established in 1996, the National Domestic Violence Hotline is a 24-hour toll-free hotline that provides crisis intervention, information, and referrals to victims of domestic violence, perpetrators, friends, and families.

The National Resource Center on Domestic Violence
3605 Vartan Way, Suite 101, Harrisburg, PA 17112
800-537-2238 ext. 5
www.nrcdv.org
The National Resource Center on Domestic Violence has been in operation since 1993. The center provides technical assistance and training, develops resource materials, and works on special projects related to domestic violence.

Source Notes

Chapter 1. A Murderous Rage

1. "911 Tapes Released From Deadly Delavan Shooting." *Channel3000.com*. Internet Broadcasting Systems, Inc., 12 June 2007. Web. 12 Dec. 2010.

2. Ibid.

3. Ibid.

4. Greg J. Borowski and John Diedrich. "6 killed in Delavan home." *JSOnline*. Journal Sentinel Inc., 11 June 2007. Web. 12 Dec. 2010.

5. "911 Tapes Released From Deadly Delavan Shooting." *Channel3000.com*. Internet Broadcasting Systems, Inc., 12 June 2007. Web. 12 Dec. 2010.

6. Dianne Feinstein. "Domestic Violence in America." *United States Senator Diane Feinstein*. N.p., 6 Oct. 2004. Web. 26 Jan. 2011.

Chapter 2. The Origins of Domestic Violence

1. K. J. Wilson. *When Violence Begins at Home*. Alameda, CA: Hunter House, 2006. Print. 315.

2. Ibid. 322.

3. Beirne Stedman. "Right of Husband to Chastise Wife." *The Virginia Law Register* 3.4 (1917): 241–248. Print. *JSTOR*. Web. 26 Jan. 2011.

Chapter 3. The Victims

1. "Champion E-newsletter 1.2, Journeys of Survival: Julie J." *Domestic Violence Resource Center*. Domestic Violence Resource Center, July 2007. Web. 14 Dec. 2010.

Chapter 4. The Abusers

1. "Commission on Domestic Violence: Survey of Recent Statistics." *American Bar Association*. American Bar Association, n.d. Web. 20 Dec. 2010.

2. Patricia Tjaden and Nancy Thoennes. "Stalking in America: Findings from the National Violence Against Women Survey." *National Criminal Justice Reference Service*. N.p., Apr. 1998. Web. 26 Jan. 2011.

3. "Facts About Domestic Violence." *Center Against Rape & Domestic Violence*. N.p., n.d. Web. 20 Dec. 2010.

Chapter 5. Lasting Effects
   1. National Resource Center on Domestic Violence. "Children Exposed to Intimate Partner Violence." *National Online Resource Center on Violence Against Women*. VAWnet, Mar. 2002. Web. 26 Jan. 2009.
   2. "Dating Abuse: Fast Facts." *loveisrespect.org*. Love is respect—National Teen Dating Abuse Helpline, Mar. 2006. Web. 22 Dec. 2010.
   3. "The Facts on Teens and Dating Violence." *Family Violence Prevention Fund*. Family Violence Prevention Fund, 2009. Web. 22 Dec. 2010.
   4. "Real Teens Talk." *Love Is Not Abuse*. Liz Claiborne, Inc., n.d. Web. 22 Dec. 2010.

Chapter 6. A Global Issue
   1. "Child Maltreatment." *World Health Organization*. WHO, Aug. 2010. Web. 27 Dec. 2010.
   2. "Declaration on the Elimination of Violence against Women." *United Nations General Assembly*. N.p., 20 Dec. 1993. Web. 27. Dec. 2010.
   3. "Gender, women and health: Violence against women by intimate partners." *World Health Organization*. WHO, n.d. Web. 26 Jan. 2011.

Chapter 7. Law Enforcement and the Legal System
None.

Chapter 8. Advocacy and Legislation
   1. William L. Hart et al. "Family Violence: Attorney General's Task Force Final Report." N.p., Sept. 1984. *Education Resources Information Center*. Web. 28 Dec. 2010.
   2. "Key Senate Committee Passes *I-VAWA*." *Family Violence Prevention Fund*. Family Violence Prevention Fund, 14 Dec. 2010. Web. 29 Dec. 2010.

Source Notes Continued

Chapter 9. Breaking the Cycle

1. "Census 2009 Report: Domestic Violence Counts 2009." *National Network to End Domestic Violence*. National Network to End Domestic Violence, 2010. Web. 30 Dec. 2010.

2. Shelly Jackson et al. "Batterer Intervention Programs: Where Do We Go From Here?" *National Criminal Justice Reference Service*. N.p., Jun. 2003. Web. 30. Dec. 2010.

Index

acquired immunodeficiency syndrome, 49
Analco, Ambrosio, 8–10
Analco, Argenis, 7, 8
Analco, Isaiah, 7, 8
Analco, Jasmine, 7, 8, 10
Aristotle, 18
arrest policies, 68–73
   See also law enforcement response

battered woman syndrome, 48
battered women's movement, 23–24
"bride price," 17–18, 60

Center Against Rape and Domestic Violence, 40
Chamberlain, P., 49
Child Abuse Prevention and Treatment Act, 80
civil rights movement, 23
Cobbe, Frances Power, 19
cyberstalking, 83
cycle of abuse, 33, 37–39, 40–42, 44, 48, 50, 84, 87, 93, 94

dating violence, 52, 53, 94
Day of Unity, 9
domestic violence
   advocacy, 9, 14, 20, 24, 76, 77–78, 81, 87–88, 89, 90, 91
   definition, 10–14
   and the elderly, 11, 12–13, 14, 26–27, 31–32, 34, 39, 47, 48, 94
   legislation, 9, 14, 24, 76, 80–84
   and male victims, 24, 37, 40
   prevention, 79, 80, 83, 87, 93–94
   and same-sex relationships, 37, 71, 92
Domestic Violence Awareness Month, 9
Domestic Violence Resource Center, 32

Family Violence Prevention and Services Act, 80, 81
Feinstein, Dianne, 12
feminism, 19, 20, 23, 24

Index Continued

global domestic violence, 13, 56–64
    bride burning, 60–61
    early marriage, 59
    female genital mutilation, 61, 62, 84
    forced prostitution, 59–60
    honor killings, 61–62
    infanticide, 58, 59
    selective abortion, 58, 59
Goldman, Ronald, 81

Hayek, Salma, 77
help for victims
    counseling, 80, 87, 89, 90, 91
    crisis intervention, 87, 90
    hotlines, 9, 24, 73, 79, 80, 84, 87–89
    shelters, 24, 30, 33, 73, 77, 80, 81, 84, 87, 88, 89–91
    support groups, 90, 91, 92
House, Erin H., 67
Huerta, Ashley Lynn, 7, 8, 10
Huerta, Gaspar, 7, 10
Huerta, Jose, 8
Huerta, Victor, 8
human immunodeficiency virus, 49

immigrant communities in the United States, 62–64
International Violence Against Women Act, 83
Iverson, Vanessa L., 7, 10

Kerry, John, 83

law enforcement response, 67–68, 69
    See also arrest policies
Laws and Customs of Beauvais, The, 18

Marin Institute, 43
Matrimonial Causes Act of 1878, 19
McAffee, Nicole Marie, 7, 8–10
McBride, Martina, 77
Mill, John Stuart, 22
Minneapolis Domestic Violence Experiment, 68–69
Ms. magazine, 9

National Center for Victims of Crime, 81
National Coalition Against Domestic Violence, 9, 11, 24, 42, 48, 49
National Crime Victimization Survey, 44
National Domestic Violence Hotline, 33, 77, 80, 87
National Network to End Domestic Violence, 88–89
National Violence Against Women Survey, 37, 47

patriarchy, 16–17, 18, 20
post-traumatic stress disorder, 51–52
protection orders, 67, 73–74, 83

rehabilitation for batterers, 87, 91–93
Reid, J., 49
"Remember My Name," 9
restraining order. *See* protection orders

sexually transmitted infections, 49, 53
signs of abuse, 11, 12, 14, 24, 33–34, 67, 93
Simpson, Nicole Brown, 81
Simpson, O. J., 81
"skimmington," 24
stalking, 38
Start Strong, 94
State v. Jesse Black, 23
Subjection of Women, The, 22
substance abuse, 42–44, 67, 74, 92

Thurman, Tracey, 78
Thurman v. City of Torrington, 78
types of abuse
  digital, 28, 53
  emotional, 11–12, 13, 27, 32, 38, 48, 53, 57, 62, 93
  financial, 13, 27–28, 34
  physical, 11, 12, 13, 22, 28, 29, 32, 34, 38, 40, 47, 48, 53, 57, 60, 62, 67, 92, 93
  rape, 11, 29–30, 48–49, 50
  sexual, 11, 12, 13, 29–30, 32, 46, 48–49, 50, 52–53, 57, 60, 62, 82
  verbal, 14, 27, 67

United Nations Declaration on the Elimination of Violence Against Women, 58

Victims of Crime Act, 80–81
Vindication of the Rights of Woman, A, 20
Violence Against Women Act, 81–83, 87

Walker, Lenore E., 48
WHO Multi-Country Study on Women's Health and Domestic Violence, 60
"Wife Torture in England," 19
Wollstonecraft, Mary, 20
Women's Advocates, 89
World Health Organization, 57, 59

About the Author

Karen Latchana Kenney is a freelance author and editor from Minneapolis, Minnesota. She has written more than 60 educational books on topics ranging from life in the Middle Ages to the issue of illegal immigration. Her books have received positive reviews in *Booklist*, *Library Media Connection*, and *School Library Journal*.

Photo Credits

Idaho Press-Tribune/Mike Vogt/AP Images, cover, 3; Pat Carter/AP Images, 6; Ed Reinke/AP Images, 13; Duane Laverty/AP Images, 15; Hulton Archive/Getty Images, 16, 21, 22, 96 (top), 97; Evening Standard/Getty Images, 25, 96 (bottom); AP Images, 26, 35, 72; Nell Redmond/AP Images, 29; Matt Smith/AP Images, 36; Shutterstock Images, 43; Jimmy May/AP Images, 45; Andy Burriss/AP Images, 46; James Gregg/Arizona Daily Star/AP Images, 51; Tom Williams/Roll Call/Getty Images, 55; Warrick Page/Edit/Getty Images, 56; PR Newswire/AP Images, 63, 99 (bottom); Jack Guez/AFP/Getty Images, 65; Ted S. Warren/AP Images, 66; Alan Ward/AP Images, 70; Steven Senne/AP Images, 75; HO/PR Newswire/AP Images, 76; Eric Draper/AP Images, 82, 99 (top); Chris Maddaloni/Roll Call/Getty Images, 85, 98; Brian Branch-Price/AP Images, 86; Harry Cabluck/AP Images, 88; Patrick Schneider/AP Images, 95